Josef Braun

A Little ABC
of the Church Interior

A Little ABC
of the
Church Interior

Josef Braun

Translated by
Linda M. Maloney

A Liturgical Press Book

THE LITURGICAL PRESS
Collegeville, Minnesota

Cover design by Ann Blattner. Reims Cathedral, 1290.

Originally published in Germany under the title *Kleines ABC des Kirchenraumes,* © 1993 by Verlag Herder, Freimburg im Breisgau. All rights reserved.

© 1997 by The Order of St. Benedict, Inc., Collegeville, Minnesota 56321. Printed in the United States of America.

ISBN 0-8146-2413-8

Do you know . . .

. . . how to tell whether someone depicted in the church is a "saint"?
. . . why there are still candles in the church, even though we now have electricity?
. . . why so many churches face East?
. . . why there is not always "fresh water" in the baptismal font?
. . . why . . . ?

In this guide to the church interior you can learn more about these things and about many other objects that make up the interior furnishings of a church.

Welcome to Our Church!

This house of God, like others, has its own history and its special artistic treasures. Like every house, it has walls, a roof, windows and doors, places to sit, and a "table." And yet there is a lot more here, and some of it is rather mysterious! We will be happy to have you join us on a tour of exploration to find those other things. This *Little ABC of the Church Interior* will guide you on your tour. It gives you some important information about the furnishings of a church interior and about the history and meaning of these objects. We will appreciate it if you are thoughtful of the people who are visiting this place for worship, to pray, or simply to sit in the silence.

Altar **A**

The high altar stands alone, close to the nave, or main part of the church. It assumes an elevated and central place because it is a symbol for Christ, and what happens on the altar is of the highest importance for the life of the Christian community.

The altar is the "table" on which, at the eucharistic meal, bread and wine are transformed into the body and blood of Christ, so that Christ becomes present in those forms and is available to be received by the faithful.

The former high altar, to the extent that it is still present, is found near the back of the choir, or chancel. It is sometimes used as an auxiliary altar where the sacred species are reserved in the tabernacle for veneration.

There were and are altars in many religions. They serve primarily as places for sacrifice, and thus for the union of God and human persons.

To begin with, the early Christians used movable wooden tables on which they placed bread and wine for the eucharistic celebration, resembling Jesus' Last Supper with his disciples. Beginning in the fourth century there was an increasing use of fixed tables made of stone.

As early as the New Testament, the metaphors used to describe Christ included "rock" and "cornerstone." Hence people saw the stone altar as a clearer symbol of Christ. It is still the custom today for at least the central portion of the altar surface to be made of natural stone.

In early Christian times many altars were built directly over the graves of the martyrs. Within or beneath the altar relics (portions of the bodies of the saints) were preserved. These relics of the saints were put in place when the altar was consecrated, and this is still done today, if possible.

Over the centuries the construction of numerous side altars led to a vast increase in the number of altars in a church. Beginning in the early Middle Ages, the chancel (the space containing the altar) was separated from the nave by a barrier and was reserved for priests and monks; the high altar was moved closer to the back of the chancel. In the following centuries this change in the placement of the altar led to a fundamental alteration in its appearance and construction. Carved or painted altarpieces were erected on the altar, and in some places there were monumental constructions above the altar that, in fact, served to dim the symbolism of the altar as the table of Christ.

While even at an early time there were crosses behind, alongside, or above the altar, the crucifix on the altar itself can only be traced to the eleventh century. The same is true of the candlesticks, the number of which was regulated by the rank of the different feast days. Today the crucifix and candles can be placed on the altar or near it. The altar cloth has its roots in the ancient and biblical custom of covering the altar, the "holy table," with linen when it was used for worship. Like the candles, it contributes to the solemn and festal character of the celebration.

In restoring the Mass to the high altar, Vatican Council II followed the original tradition: the altar is once again the "table" around which the community can gather and on which nothing is to be placed except those things necessary for the eucharistic celebration.

> Make this altar a sign of Christ from whose pierced side flowed blood and water, which ushered in the sacraments of the Church. Make it a table of joy, where the friends of Christ may hasten to cast upon you [God] their burdens and cares and take up their journey restored. Make it a place of communion and peace, so that those who share the body and blood of your Son may be filled with his Spirit and grow in your life of love. Make it a source of unity and friendship, where your people may gather as one. . . . Make it the center of our praise and thanksgiving until we arrive at the eternal tabernacle, where, together with Christ, high priest and living altar, we will offer you an everlasting sacrifice of praise.
>
> From the Prayer for the Consecration of an Altar

Ambo

The ambo is the lectern from which, during the Liturgy of the Word at Mass, the readings, responsorial psalm, gospel, homily, and prayers of the people are read or spoken.

In order to emphasize its importance and that of the gospel, the ambo is often made very large and is given a place of honor near the altar. This is meant to express the fact that Christ gives himself in two ways: in the words of proclamation at the ambo and in the sacrament of the Eucharist at the altar.

Over time the place within the church from which the word is proclaimed has often changed. In many churches there is still a pulpit fixed to a pillar or to the wall serving as an elevated place for preaching. It is basket-shaped and is furnished with a staircase and a sound-reflecting top; in most cases it is richly decorated. Beginning in the fifteenth century such pulpits became the rage almost everywhere, and they often shifted far back into the nave, a long distance from the altar. With the liturgical reforms of Vatican Council II, the pulpit lost its function. The tradition of the ambo was revived, and it was given a place close to the congregation and to the altar, permitting direct eye contact between the congregation and the person at the ambo.

The word "gospel" comes from Old English, but its Latin equivalent, *evangelium,* is reflected in the English word "evangel," and in many words such as "evangelist." All these come from the Greek *euangélion,* meaning "good news" or "glad tidings." The ambo, as the place of proclamation, especially of the gospel, is the place within the church from which this good news of Jesus is communicated to human beings.

Angel

Angels are usually depicted with wings and sometimes also with a shining light surrounding them. They wear white garments as a sign of their purity and have a halo or nimbus around their heads.

Images of angels can be found in different parts of the church, some combined with an object or a figure (for example, Christ, Mary, the saints) or in a scene depicted in a window, an altarpiece, or a fresco. Thus they can be found as watchers at the door or at a grave, as conquerors of the Evil One (the archangel Michael), as servants of God, Christ, and Mary, as protectors (the archangel Raphael), as bearers of symbolic and liturgical objects, as musicians, and—often with words painted on a ribbon—as proclaimers and interpreters of a message (the archangel Gabriel).

Images of angels have been part of the decoration of churches from early Christian times. Over the centuries the most varied kinds of angels have appeared, and the places where they are found and the meaning they convey have changed. The depiction of angels was strongly influenced not only by biblical narratives and legends but also by the idea that the church and the worship conducted in it are an image here on earth of the heavenly Jerusalem and the heavenly liturgy. Added to this was the belief that the angels are present at the Church's worship and cooperate in it. Thus the angels are signs of heavenly glory and models of true adoration.

Angels are not only artistic decoration; they are meant to convey a "message," to strengthen faith in God's mysterious activity in the world, and to encourage us to united praise of God.

Apostle Candles

In most older Catholic churches there are twelve candleholders in the nave, which are attached to the walls or pillars. Crosses are usually fixed or carved close to them. The twelve candles are lighted on the feast of the church's dedication and on the principal feasts of the Church year. They are to remind the people that the faith of every congregation rests on the witness of the twelve apostles. Those twelve were also the first whom Jesus commanded to be "light" for the world.

Baptismal Font   B

The structure that contains the baptismal water is called the baptismal font; it is the place of baptism. Because this is usually done in the parish of the one being baptized, every parish church must have a baptismal font. In older churches it is usually placed close to the chancel, or else in a separate baptismal chapel. Ordinarily, it is made of stone or metal (bronze), and may be

 found in a variety of forms (for example, in shapes resembling a cup, a bowl, a kettle, or a shell). A cover is often used to protect the baptismal water in the font from dirt. Sometimes the baptismal font has ornamental decorations and carvings representing the events of salvation history.

The baptismal water blessed during the Easter Vigil is usually kept in the baptismal font throughout the Easter season; at other times, the water is specially blessed before each baptism in order to clarify for those assembled the meaning of baptism, which is expressed in the words of the prayer for the blessing of baptismal water.

Early Christian baptism originally took place wherever flowing or standing water was available. With the transfer of baptism to the interior of the churches, special places, or even separate buildings, were devised for it. In these baptismal rooms, or baptisteries, there was usually a basin or pool (piscina) for the baptismal water. People who came to be baptized walked down into the basin and had water poured over them. When the practice of infant baptism became general and when, from the sixth century onward, the right to baptize was transferred from the bishops' churches to the parishes, it became customary to provide elevated fonts for baptism, since the basin in the floor proved to be poorly adapted to the baptism of infants.

The baptismal font has a special place within the church interior; it is placed so that baptism, which incorporates new members into the community of the faithful, can take place in view of the whole congregation.

The baptismal font reminds the faithful of baptism and its meaning: their belonging to Christ and the Church, the fulfillment of their lives in Christ, their mission as witnesses to God, and their call to new life.

Bells

Among the things belonging to many churches, especially older churches, are the bell near the sacristy, the hand bells near the altar, and the great bell or bells in the church tower.

The sacristy bell signals, for those inside the church, that the worship service is about to begin. The small hand bells at the altar can be used to draw attention to especially significant parts of the liturgical celebration (for example, the consecration at Mass or the procession or blessing with the Blessed Sacrament).

Bells in a tower have been widespread since the eighth century. Beginning approximately in the thirteenth century their size and tone quality began to improve and their numbers to increase. They are blessed for their office, and they can be rung—primarily for church purposes—singly, in groups, or in their full complement. Besides ringing before the beginning of worship, they can be sounded for funerals, processions, and at the turn of the year. The bell rung in the morning, at midday, and in the evening is intended to call the faithful to prayer (the so-called Angelus), recalling the incarnation of Jesus. In addition, it should call everyone to stop and reflect at these particular times of day and to redirect their lives on these occasions.

The bells contribute to the dignified process and the festive nature of liturgical celebrations. Their message is directed to the people, inviting them to private prayer and to community worship.

Candles

C

Candles contribute to the festive atmosphere and, for example when they are placed before images of Mary and the saints, serve as symbols of the blessings extended by God. At least two candles burn on or near the altar during worship.

In many churches there is also a stand for votive candles, where people may employ candles as a way of expressing their needs, their prayers, and their thanksgiving toward God.

Light drives out darkness, orients us, gives us warmth, confidence, and life. The natural light of a candle conveys this more impressively than artificial light, and it is highly valued for that reason. Especially for special events that interrupt the daily routine (birthday parties, for example) we turn to "natural sources of light." In the Church and in our religious lives also, candles play a central role at the high points of the Church year (for example, the Easter candle and the candles on the Advent wreath and  on the Christmas tree). This is also true of important events in a Christian's life (for example, the baptismal and First Communion candles and others used at weddings, wakes, and funerals).

Candles are a symbol of Christ, the "light of the world," who overcame the darkness of death through his resurrection. They are a sign of hope, joy, and life. When candles burn, consuming their wax, they should remind us of the self-giving love of God.

They are meant to encourage us, too, to be "light" that enlightens the lives of other people. (See also Apostle Candles, Sanctuary Lamp, and Easter Candle.)

Choir Stalls

In cathedrals, monastic churches, and in some older parish churches there are rows of wooden seats for clerics and monks, placed usually along the sides of the chancel. They are called "choir stalls," and are frequently provided with a high back and a good deal of carving.

These seats may be open or may be separated by intervening partitions; usually the seat itself can be folded up. The provision of arm rests, kneelers, and supports for the buttocks attached to the underside of the seat (called "misericordias") to relieve fatigue in standing all served to lighten long periods in the stalls.

The choir stalls served the priests or monks when they joined in praise of God at the Liturgy of the Hours and during the singing at Mass. They are still used for those purposes today in many places.

Church

Obviously, God's presence in the world is not limited to churches. The earliest Christians were already aware that God has no need of temples and sanctuaries built by human hands.

The "house" appropriate to the God of Christians is the human heart. God can be present wherever people open themselves to unity with God and other human beings. But the presence of God is not at human disposal; it is a gift. This gift of the presence of God is promised to the community that gathers in the name of Christ. Especially when they come together to celebrate the Eucharist, to pray, to administer the sacraments, and to celebrate the mysteries of faith, they are certain of the presence of the Lord. The church, as the place of assembly, creates an atmosphere by means of its signs and symbols that promotes Christians' inner recollection, strengthens them in faith, and opens them to an encounter with God. In some churches there is a vestibule, or narthex, at the entrance that begins to prepare the faithful for the atmosphere of the worship space.

The principal part of the church is divided into the nave and the chancel; it thus reflects the structure of the assembled community with its head (chancel) and members (nave). The chancel is elevated several steps above the level of the nave, or else it is emphasized by special decoration. The altar, ambo, and presider's chair are located there. The nave and all other parts of the church are ordered toward the chancel. No matter what its special structure, every church constitutes a unified whole, reflecting the unity of the congregation.

The arrangement of many churches, with the altar to the east, goes back to the stance for prayer in antiquity: the person praying faced toward the rising sun. This posture was taken up by Christians because they thought of Christ as the new "sun" who gives true life, and they expected Christ to return from the east.

The greatest possible variety of styles, materials, devotional ideals, liturgical and theological ideas, has shaped the design of churches through the ages and has produced very different types of churches. Thus churches with long central naves are more clearly an expression of the pilgrim status of human beings on journey toward God, while rounded or centrally focused forms express human dwelling with God.

The church not only serves the congregational assembly for worship; it is open to all who seek it as a place of prayer, reflection, silence, and security or for the sake of its artistic decoration. The church, as a place of encounter with God, is a mysterious place, one that commands respect and reverence. Here human beings can meet God, who as host receives them, gives them gifts, strengthens them, consoles them, transforms them, and sends them forth into the world.

Confessional

The confessionals, or reconciliation rooms, are located on the sides or near the back of the church, either in the main part or in a side chapel (sometimes called the confession chapel).

For many centuries the confession of sins was made publicly in the church at the chair (cathedra) of the bishop or, later, of the priest. This very prominent seat of the confessor was the earliest form of the confessional. In the wake of the Catholic reform movements of the sixteenth century, it developed into a fixed structure, usually in three parts and more or less enclosed. The priest occupied the central section, which was divided on each side from the penitent's place by a wall pierced by a grille or screen. This provided better conditions for anonymous confession.

In recent times, the reconciliation room with its personal atmosphere offers a spatial alternative for confession and spiritual direction. The sacrament of reconciliation achieves just that: reconciliation with God. Therefore the confessional and reconciliation room are places of repentance, renewal, and a new beginning that is the gift of God.

Cross

The cross is the central Christian symbol. If it has an image of the crucified Christ on it, it is called a "crucifix." It is a confessional symbol and an object of meditation and veneration.

The altar cross takes pride of place over all other images of the cross within the church. It may hang above the altar or be placed on the wall behind the altar or in a stand nearby.

The elevated position of the altar cross is meant to illustrate that all the liturgical actions in the church take place beneath this sign of salvation. Its proximity to the altar should make clear that Christ gives himself at the eucharistic celebration on human altars just as he did in surrendering himself in sacrifice on the cross. Many objects in the church (side altars, tabernacle, baptismal font, holy water font, etc.) may be decorated with a cross in order to indicate the religious purpose of the object, the state of belonging to Christ, and the blessing of God that is here at work. It can be very informative simply to investigate the number and placement of crosses in a church!

The cross may appear alone or as part of a scene or image, usually connected with the passion of Jesus. It is quite often found as an attribute with images of the saints to demonstrate their devotion and their special relationship to the cross.

The cross was used in churches for a long time without the addition of the image, or "corpus," of the crucified Jesus. As a next stage, Christ was shown on the cross as the Living One, triumphant over death, a divine victor with open eyes and erect posture. Finally, in the High Middle Ages (since about the twelfth century) the image of the crucified Jesus, suffering or dead, became dominant. It served to emphasize the humanity of Jesus.

The cross can be found, and has been found for millennia, in the widest variety of cultural contexts, as an abstract sign, and with a wide spectrum of symbolic meanings. For Christians, it only received its significance through the resurrection of Jesus; it became the sign of Christ's victory over sin, suffering, and death and thus a visible sign of redemption. It is the image of the solidarity of Christ with all who suffer and die. Finally, the cross always points to Christ himself, who, like the beams of the cross, can join everything into one: God and humanity, human beings with one another, and individual human beings with themselves.

Easter Candle E

During the Easter season an especially large, decorated candle is placed on a candle stand in the chancel and is kept burning during worship. During the remainder of the Church year it stands near the baptismal font, because when people are baptized, their baptismal candles are lighted from it.

The Easter candle, or "Paschal candle," is traced to the ancient Church's celebration of the Easter Vigil. It is decorated with the first and last letters of the Greek alphabet (alpha and omega), and with the number of the year. These are signs of the power and glory of the risen Christ, yesterday, today, and forever. The five red wax nails inserted in the form of a cross recall Jesus' wounds.

During the celebration of Jesus' resurrection at the Easter Vigil the candle is blessed and lighted from the new Easter fire. The celebrant says, "May the light of Christ risen in glory scatter the darkness of heart and mind."

After that, the candle, as symbol of the resurrection of Christ, is carried into the darkened church, and the candles of the faithful are lighted from its flame. This illustrates Jesus' words: "I am the light of the world. Whoever follows me will never walk in darkness but will have the light of life" (John 8:12).

Flowers F

Flowers in the church—especially near the altar and in front of the images and statues of the saints—are an expression of respect and devotion.

They should contribute to the festive atmosphere of the church and be signs of the fullness of life that has its origin in God, the creator of the world. In their beauty they serve as an image of the present and future glory of God.

Holy Water Font H

Holy water fonts are typical signs of a Catholic church. They are placed near the entrances, and a storage vessel is also often located nearby so the faithful can take holy water for various purposes such as the sprinkling of graves and for use in their homes.

Because of its purifying, renewing, and life-giving power, water has been and is used in many religions to the present time for religious purposes, especially ritual purification and preparation for an encounter with the divine. In Christianity water is a powerful symbol: at baptism, when the priest washes his hands at Mass, and at consecrations and blessings. When it is blessed, the water is handed over to God and entrusted to God's power, with a prayer for the blessing of those persons who make use of it in faith.

In many churches it is customary to add salt when the water is blessed as another expression of the purifying effect of the water. Holy water fonts are places where every believer can recall his or her baptism (as signifying belonging to Christ and to the community of the faithful) in an especially vivid manner by signing himself or herself with the blessed water in the form of a cross, in the name of the triune God. ("In the name of the Father, and of the Son, and of the Holy Spirit.")

Holy water fonts are placed at the entrances and exits of the church so that the act of entering and leaving the house of God can be done in a deliberate and conscious manner. They invite us, when using the holy water as we enter the church, to express our inward readiness for renewal by God, and when leaving, to surrender ourselves to God's sending, leading, and protection.

Loft

Lofts are raised sections, often placed on both sides of the central nave, around the chancel, or at the back above the entrance to the church.

In Western church architecture, these lofts have multiplied since the Romanesque period, reaching their high point during the baroque era.

Lofts were reserved for particular groups (nuns, men, the nobility) or for special purposes (organ loft, architectonic decoration, etc.).

Today the loft usually serves as a place for the choir, the organ, and part of the congregation.

Mary   M

Mary, the mother of Jesus, is honored above all other saints in the Catholic Church's liturgy and popular piety.

Her image is found in every church in a special place of honor. There is often a side altar dedicated to Mary, and it may be richly decorated with candles and flowers.

It is frequently the case that candles burn near her images, because the faithful love to call on her as an advocate.

Many churches are named for her and have her as their patron.

Mary is usually portrayed as a young woman, in some countries dressed in a red gown and a blue mantle. One finds her in individual images, but she also forms part of scenes from her life, the life of Jesus, and the Marian legends.

In the course of history a great many symbols were assigned to her (for example, the sun, the moon, a crown with twelve stars, the rosary), all of them intended to describe her nature, her virtues, and her significance. Among the almost infinite variety of depictions of Mary, the following (among others) are frequently to be found: Mary with the child Jesus (the Madonna), the Mother of Sorrows (with the body of Jesus), the Madonna with the protecting mantle, and the Queen of Heaven.

The images of Mary are intended to encourage devotion to her as the mother of God, the mother of the Savior. Mary is outstanding as an advocate. As a model of faith and an image of the Church she encourages us to trust in God at all times and with our whole being.

Because she has the closest and most intimate possible connection to Jesus Christ, she is a sign that points beyond herself to the Son of God.

Organn   O

The organ, with its many pipes sounded by air from a bellows, is usually found near the rear of the church or close to the chancel; it is frequently placed in a loft. It gradually gained access to the churches, although until the eleventh century it was regarded as a profane instrument used for court ceremonies. In the thirteenth century it became a regular practice to install organs in all important churches. Today an organ is part of the furnishing of most churches.

With its variety and fullness of sound, the organ contributes to the glorification of God. The reflective and festive atmosphere it creates opens the hearts of the faithful to common and unified praise of God.

Presider's Chair ## P

The somewhat outsized or elevated chair for the presider is usually placed at one side of the chancel or in the apex of the space.

This chair for the presider and those for the assistants at worship are collectively called "sedilia."

From earliest times sitting on a special elevated chair was regarded as an honor and a mark of distinction; it was a sign of a corresponding position and set of duties within the community.

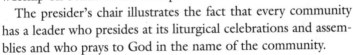

The original seat for the one who presided at the eucharistic celebration was the bishop's "cathedra" (from the Greek word *cathédra*, a chair). Since the fourth century a presider's chair has also been customarily provided for the priest who leads worship on behalf of the bishop.

The presider's chair illustrates the fact that every community has a leader who presides at its liturgical celebrations and assemblies and who prays to God in the name of the community.

Sacristy

The sacristy is a room near the chancel of the church that is used in preparing for the material aspects of worship (for example, donning liturgical robes) and for internal recollection by those who exercise a liturgical office. This is also the place for the vessels, books, and robes that are needed for the worship services.

Saints

As a rule, the most common sign of a saint's portrait is the halo or nimbus around the head. Additional attributes may point to special traits or virtues of the saint or to real or legendary events in the saint's life.

Even though the saints no longer live among us but with God, as friends of God and humanity they remain close to us in love, and they can be called upon to speak for us.

When saints, after their death, are recognized (canonized) by the Church, their memorial can be celebrated in the liturgy of the entire Church. The images and statues of saints have an honored place in the church building. This is especially true of the images of the saint or saints to whose care the church has been dedicated (patron saints). Frequently a side altar is dedicated to the patron saint or saints.

Besides the saints who enjoy widespread favor in popular piety, there are often images of the saints whose relics are preserved in the church, usually in its altars. There may also be images of saints who are honored by practitioners of particular trades or crafts in the region, or those who were active in the diocese in which the church is located.

The saints lived their love for God and neighbor in an outstanding fashion. As models of trust in God, they encourage us to discover our own calling and to live it fully.

Sanctuary Lamp

The red or clear glass lamp that is always burning near the tabernacle is often regarded as the typical mark of a Catholic church.

It is a part of ancient tradition that a light should be kept burning at holy places as a sign of reverence and a symbol of the blessing that emanates from the place. In Christian churches, too, from the beginning there were lights at the tombs of the martyrs and in front of the altars. Beginning in about the thirteenth century, with the increasing emergence of a practice of venerating the reserved Eucharist, there arose a custom of keeping an "eternal light" burning before the tabernacle containing the sacred host.

Burning day and night, this light symbolizes the enduring sacramental presence of Christ in the eucharistic bread in the tabernacle and is a sign of God's closeness and God's love for human beings.

Stations of the Cross

The Stations of the Cross are a sequence of pictures or carvings, usually fourteen in number, depicting the story of Jesus' passion, beginning with his condemnation by Pilate and ending with his being placed in the tomb. Occasionally there is a fifteenth station, the resurrection. As a rule the stations are numbered, and each is surmounted by a cross.

The Stations of the Cross originated in the pilgrims' custom of following the route of Jesus' passion when they made pilgrimages to Jerusalem.

In the late Middle Ages meditations on the Stations of the Cross took the place of pilgrimage to the Holy Land; for this purpose the various stages along the way of the cross were devised as a substitute. In this way Jesus' last journey could be followed in one's own locality, and his suffering could be visualized in a more vivid way.

Series of pictures or carvings representing the Stations of the Cross were first placed in and near monastic churches, on high places, and at pilgrimage sites. Around the end of the seventeenth and beginning of the eighteenth century they were moved to the interior of the parish churches, and they became more and more widespread. Of the fourteen stations that were generally adopted, eight have a direct foundation in the Gospels. The others (Jesus' falling three times under the weight of the cross, his meeting with Mary, the episode with Veronica's veil, and the body of Jesus lying in his mother's lap) were derived from popular piety or originated in legend.

The Stations of the Cross play a special part in the Lenten observance. In the so-called meditation of the stations, a person "follows" Jesus' route to his death, praying and contemplating those events. The Stations of the Cross are not meant to be a reminiscence of Jesus' suffering. Instead, by calling attention to the solidarity of Jesus with all who suffer and to his overcoming of suffering, they are meant to strengthen us so that we will not repress our own and other's suffering but acknowledge it and cooperate in overcoming it.

Tabernacle   T

There is a tabernacle in every church where the Eucharist is celebrated. As a sign that Christ is present there in a special way, a red or clear lamp burns near the tabernacle: this is the sanctuary lamp, or "eternal light." Because the holy sacrament is preserved in this little cabinet it can be locked, and it is usually richly decorated. It enjoys an honorable place on a side altar or in a sacrament chapel. It may stand on a separate column within the chancel, or it may be inserted in a wall; in some places it is kept on the former high altar.

The place and form of reservation changed frequently over the centuries. The placement of the tabernacle on the altar and its association with the altar itself were customary in Italy as early as the sixteenth century. In Germany, where it was the custom for a very long time to reserve the sacred hosts in wall cabinets and little "sacrament houses," the tabernacle did not become the general rule until the eighteenth century.

The tabernacle has served since the early Christian era for preservation of consecrated hosts for the dying. From the early Middle Ages onward it was also a place for the adoration and veneration of Christ in the form of the eucharistic bread. Many of the faithful, therefore, genuflect before the tabernacle and remain there in silent prayer.

In the enduring presence of Christ in the eucharistic bread in the tabernacle, we can experience in an especially vivid way Jesus' promise: "Remember, I am with you always, to the end of the age" (Matt 28:20).

Bibliography

Fischer, Balthasar. *Signs, Words, and Gestures*. New York: Pueblo Publishing, 1981; Collegeville: The Liturgical Press, 1990.

Richter, Klemens. *The Meaning of the Sacramental Symbols*. Collegeville: The Liturgical Press, 1990.

This little book of definitions is meant to introduce youngsters or others unfamiliar with a church to the purpose and history of the altar, baptismal font, candles, sanctuary lamp, and other furnishings or parts of a church interior.

Josef Braun is a liturgist of the diocese of Regensburg in Germany.

ISBN 0-8146-2413-8

9 780814 624135

U.S. $3.95